LICENSED

DAILY PRACTICES INTO A CLOSE RELATIONSHIP WITH GOD

VAL GEORGE

WESTBOW
PRESS®
A DIVISION OF THOMAS NELSON
& ZONDERVAN

WestBow Press books may be ordered through booksellers or by contacting:

WestBow Press
A Division of Thomas Nelson & Zondervan
1663 Liberty Drive
Bloomington, IN 47403
www.westbowpress.com
1 (866) 928-1240

ISBN: 978-1-5127-7171-8 (sc)
ISBN: 978-1-5127-7172-5 (e)

Library of Congress Control Number: 2017900411

Print information available on the last page.

WestBow Press rev. date: 02/20/2017

PREFACE

Glory and honor to God because He has the perfect timing. He does not waste any of the resources He gives. He has invested in us, and His word will not come back to Him void. He established creation, redemption, and eternity. Every day, we thank Him for the salvation of our souls.

Licensed is a must read for every youth, campus student, child, single, and married. For the church, youth pastor, and summer camp director trying to reach the youth with a "grab it and go" book, *Licensed* can fit snugly in a bookbag or purse and can be read aloud to children. For that parent who thinks his prodigal child will never come home because he thinks he blew it, rest assured that God still works in mysterious ways. *Licensed* has been written to open that child's mind to practical ways in which he can speak and believe God again. For the mature individual who thinks it is too late, believe that God wants you to be fruitful whatever age you claim. The God of all flesh will renew your youth. He has promised you an abundant life. Take Him at His word. He is the Amen. Remember!

I wrote this book when I was "heavily pregnant" with ideas

for books and novels and how to reach souls for God's kingdom. I have been the editor for years of my church's bulletins and partners' newsletters. From the outpouring of the responses from partners, it showed how grateful they were for the easy reads and conversational style in which I wrote. In addition, I have countless journal entries accumulated over the years that were just collecting dust on my book shelves. Hence, with the encouragements and support of family members and friends, *Licensed* was birthed to the glory of God.

God hears and knows all we do and will ever do. He has placed His mark on His children and wants us to come to Him as we are. We all too often think that our education, skills, money, and talents earned us a place in God's hall of faith. Many of us think we have to be in church buildings to worship and praise God. However, God has wired us to have a close relationship with Him, and so He will draw closer to us, everywhere and anywhere. In our simple daily activities, practices, chores, and tasks, *Licensed* shows us how we can include and acknowledge God.

In a very simplistic way, *Licensed* shows how we can have a daily walk into a close relationship with God using activities we love to do. As we pass the torch to the next generation, they too will continue to pass on lessons learned and best practices for their daily walk with God and become more fruitful. We must put God in the center of all we do.

I would love to give God all the glory and honor for the privilege of trusting me with this project to reach souls for His kingdom. He is clearly the Author and Finisher of my faith.

He has provided me with supportive family, friends, mentees, and students who keep me on my toes, and my church family, who is always praying for me. Your names are etched in God's book for eternity. Thank you very much! *Merci beaucoup! Muchas gracias! Jesus is Lord!*

INTRODUCTION

Do you have a license? Or licenses? Your skills, whatever they are, will certainly need an endorsement and a license that seals the deal. I remember the day I drove my son to get his driving license at the ripe old age of eighteen. When he was asked to parallel park, in a split second, or so it seemed, the car was sitting like a royal prince on the assigned space.

I had to ask him how he performed that feat so effortlessly, and he simply said with a smug smile, "Skills, Mom, skills."

What are the skills you possess? You can get licenses for about anything and everything under the sun. To some, some licenses are too ridiculous for words; for others they seem to fit everything they believe. The skills you have today can be approved by the appropriate agency and a license issued thereafter. In short, you can have a license to do anything.

Wait a minute here. You mean I can do anything? Yes! All things are lawful, but not all things are profitable.

First of all, when you are asked to name a type of license, the first will be a driver's license. These days, the myriad of licenses is mind boggling. Do you know you need a license to hunt and to fish in certain areas, to name a few?

A license is more of a necessity than a luxury and spells freedom to a sixteen-year-old with a learner's permit. The headstrong feeling and euphoria a young child feels will depend on many conditions, especially if he has to help chauffer his siblings across town for games, recitals, school runs, and a myriad of other errands. The child will soon find out that there is nothing like luxury in the license he received. It is a chore that sure comes with benefits.

Also, to a veteran driver, the freedom of yesteryears has been replaced by the humdrum of everyday living. It is, after all, one errand at a time. You bet that the novelty of getting a driver's license has worn off. Life happens, and it seems to go on and on like a locomotive running on the interstate. Let us therefore move on to the business at hand.

Our premise in this chapter will be based on 1 Corinthians 2:12: "Now we have received, not the spirit of the world, but the Spirit who is from God, *so that we may know the things freely given to us by God*" (emphasis mine).

You have the license now!

The World's License Requirements

Lest I state the obvious, the license you now hold allows you freedom on the streets and highways for as long as you are capable and deemed responsible.

What are the requirements for a driver's license? You need a social security number for those in the United States, as well as to pass both written and road tests. Most times, it is the only form of ID that guarantees you access to do a plethora of activities like banking and going to school, to mention a couple.

For a fish lover or during deer hunting season, you need licenses to be able to enjoy these recreational activities. Whether you are married or divorced, you picked up a license at one time or another.

Before the wedding, each couple looks forward to the day they will legally be joined together as one. It spells *freedom*. Freedom from what has been a nagging question for me. When you have the answer, please tell me, dear reader. If you are contemplating getting a license today or soon, what privileges do you get from that license?

A license gives you permission, simply stated.

Guess what?

Every driver's license has an expiration date. The traditional license, as we know it, has to be renewed every so often. When you relocate, for example to another state, you are required to go down to the Department of Public Safety and register for a new one. The other caveat here is that the license itself has a lifespan of ten years. If your eyes need corrective lenses, you have to report the change. There are a lot of stipulations, you know.

His License Requirements

Here is an introduction into the world of another kind of license.

So what kind of license am I talking about? Growing up, I didn't know what commitment to Christ meant. I called myself a Christian. Little did I know that I was only deceiving myself, playing church! Where did I get off with that kind of thinking? I was so far from it that I was on another planet. Talk about women being from Venus. I was even on the dark side of Venus. God forgave my foolish ignorance. Whom was I fooling?

You know those campus Christian brothers and sisters, always touting their Bibles, smiling, and nagging you to attend their fellowship meetings. That was my impression or opinion. They were relentless in their efforts to make sure everybody stopped going to wild parties, wearing makeup, and just plain enjoying life. Boring! Again, that used to be my perspective. I used to watch their eyes mist over when they prayed. Sometimes the tears would flow down my roommates' eyes during her fellowship time with God. I used to sneer and thought she was a wimpy little sissy. I looked forward to

Friday nights because it meant freedom to party all night long. In the recesses of my mind, I had these nagging thoughts. What if my parents caught me? They were a clear four-hour drive away. There was no way they could catch me. But catch me doing what? For crying out loud, what was wrong with a little party here and there? As a confession, I only went to dance, to show off my new clothes, and of course, to get the attention of the campus boys. Never mind that I already had a boyfriend. It was simply girls trying to have some fun. Then why did I feel guilty every time I snuck back into the dorms in the early hours of the morning? I didn't care much about my sleeping roommate. She must have been praying for me all the time. She didn't push or berate me about what I wasn't doing right. I didn't drink or smoke, yet I knew my parents would have disapproved of the "freedom" that many freshman and seniors alike have abused. Coming back to campus from club hopping one early morning, one of our buddies lost his life in a car accident. I still hear the echo of his voice saying, "I don't want to die." He died anyway. Something changed among us that early morning. I, for one, decided to stop, and it was cold turkey. There was a check in my spirit that day about my future and my life. I had so many unanswered questions after that day. I thank God that I was still able to graduate from college with good grades.

And then Jesus happened. I went about my merry way for many years after college—got my license to marry, had a beautiful son whom I still adore till today, and started a teaching job at a high school. Little did I know that it was all a setup! You see, my marriage license turned to a divorce license, and my life did somersaults. Because I wanted another marriage license so badly, I hooked up with a guy who claimed to love me. The only condition for that license was if and when I had a child for him. In my naivety, I got sucked into that lie from the pit of hell. After a series of tests and technological manipulations, not to mention the financial burden, I realized that I had fallen into a depressed state. I hit rock bottom. I actually told myself that I was only complete if I had a man and children. What a backward way of thinking. Where did I place God in all these plans and more plans for how I wanted my dreams to come true? Then Jesus happened again. He met me at the bottom of the rock, and He has been my Rock ever since. I got hooked on the love of God through His benevolent Son, Jesus!

I thought born-again Christianity was stifling, a party pooper experience. To me then, God just sat in heaven "zapping" people, judging us for every infraction, punishing and killing people. I used to be scared of God, especially because we can't see Him. But I found out that you can feel Him. As Holy Spirit resides in you, you can feel God's presence. I have learned to trust Him with my whole life and in everything. He is the best thing that happened to me since sliced wheat bread. Go figure! Seriously, I am not in any way or fashion nonchalant about God extending His hand of grace to me.

He is a merciful God, you know—very rich in mercy. Once you confess that Jesus is Lord of all, you are now triumphant in Christ Jesus. You have victory in the name of Jesus. His blood makes you as white as snow. What an awesome God!

I will look you in the eye and admit that I am sold on Jesus. He is the best thing that happened to me.

How do I know that? I have the license to prove it. I thought you couldn't enjoy life. You and I were purchased the moment we confessed Jesus as Lord and Savior. You have victory in the name of Jesus. You and I are meant to reflect His glory on earth. Don't think this is too cheesy for you. It is real; He is real. Jesus is the answer! Take a moment and reflect on what I just said. You belong to Him!

Your license gives you permission to say so—not only to say so but to be the best at what you have been called to do. You have the permission to live a victorious life.

Don't you want to have a life where you can make decisions that you know will honor God? I call myself a "lazy Christian." You think I am lazy physically or otherwise? No, I just let the Lord make my decisions for me, hence the label I put on myself.

You have His license.

Do you think living happily ever after is only for fairy tales?

You can have the joy of the Lord fill your every waking moment. You can spend eternity with God. That means being forever in His presence.

Ask Him for the license today.

He will give you His peace in any and all tumultuous situations. Ask Him now!

Apply for the license right now. What are you waiting for? I want to see your beautiful picture on that ID. God has His stamp on it—endorsed for eternity. God's identification proof is your name written in the Lamb's Book of Life. I read this poem written by an anonymous author. I have personalized it, and so can you.

Dear Reader,
If God had a refrigerator, your picture would be on it.
If He had a wallet, your photo would be in it.
He sends you flowers every spring.
He sends you a sunrise every morning.
Whenever you want to talk, He listens.
He can live anywhere in the universe, but He chose your heart.
Now God didn't promise days without pain, laughter without sorrow, sun without rain, but He did promise strength for the day, comfort for the tears, and light for the way.
So face it, Reader, He is crazy about you!
Therefore, let us:
Give thanks to the Lord, for he is good; his love endures forever.
Amen. (1 Chronicles 16:34)

Benefits of a License

What are the benefits of your license?
Access to the throne room twenty-four hours a day
Contentment
Dominion

Faith
Favor
Great name
His grace
His image
Prosperity

Guess what?
His license will not expire!
You won't need to renew it. All you need to do is produce it every day wherever you go. It will open doors for you that you never could get in without His signet ring or seal of approval. Wouldn't you like to live a life where someone else is making the decisions?

I do, and it's comforting to know. I just asked Him to take the reins or the wheel of your car, so you better move over right now and let Him drive. I like the end of every trip, the great outcome every day. He knows the curves and turns and even where that police officer is waiting to give you a friendly warning or maybe a ticket. You see, beloved, He has promised to be with you everywhere you go. He was with Abraham, Isaac, and Jacob, so He will never leave you or abandon you to go on this journey by yourself. He has your license plate number etched in His mind. Let God drive today.

Do you remember birthdays and holidays in your home? I remember buying birthday gifts for my family, especially my son. He tore into his gifts with gusto. However, at the end of the day, when the novelty of the gift wore off, the gifts would be among the pile of "has seen better days." I even remember one year when he received a new pair of tennis shoes that he had coveted for many weeks. Finally when the gift was unwrapped, he slept in those shoes for days. That too ended up in the ...yes, you guessed it,,, at the back of his closet and eventually given away since his feet grew.

All right, so I exaggerate. Tell me sincerely where you threw your last birthday gift. You don't even remember what it looks like anymore. Or did you trade it for something more to your liking? *God has a tailor-made gift for you!*

Yet Almighty God, your Father, is simply telling you that every gift you will ever desire is in His warehouse. He even has a steady supply of all the licenses you will ever need.

So put out your empty baskets and get ready to fill them up. He waits. This is an all-you-can-carry buffet line. Fill up till you are overflowing. What are you waiting for?

My baskets are full to overflowing. I have all the licenses I need for daily living.. At every stage in my journey, He teaches me what I need. I applied when I accepted His Son as Lord and Savior. So anytime I need a license, I pull out my bowl, like Oliver Twist, and with a pout and a dimpled smile, I ask for more. He never fails to fill me to overflowing.

Your Part—Requirements

This is so simple, and yet many can't or won't think about applying. Dear reader, you won't need a pen and paper. You don't need a test to see how roadworthy you are. Nobody will take you on a road inspection or test ride before you qualify for a license.

Allow your heart to say yes to God.

Give Him your heart today. Don't look around you to see who is talking to you. God is talking to you through your inner man called your spirit.

Hear Him calling your name. You can answer to Him right now. You have everything to gain and nothing to lose.

So what kind of license do you want to apply for? Check out the list, and mark any one you need. You can be greedy and select as many as you want. Actually, be greedy and grab as many as you want. Ready, set, *go!*

Whose Inadequacies—Deal with Them

So you think you don't qualify for a license?

This book intends to help everyone who has struggled with any of the following feelings:

- uneasiness—the joy of the Lord is your strength
- hopelessness—there is hope in Jesus
- debilitating debts—cut up those credit cards
- crippling diseases—the healing power of God is working in you; the blood of Jesus is now flowing through you spiritually.
- generational curses—you are blessed
- discouragement—get a massage
- promotion that you didn't get—you are a rising star
- divorce—there is a silver lining
- raising rebellious teenagers—the young shall grow
- overdue term paper—just do it
- paying back taxes owed—cough it up
- caring for aging parents—you will be old one day too
- going round in circles—stay in one place

Sounds familiar, doesn't it? Whatever your struggles are, you can rise above every situation in the name of Jesus. The quagmire is not new under the sun. This book is for fighters—fighters who have what it takes to overcome every setback.

You have prayed and prayed.

You are fighting for your family (worth it).

What do you have to lose? You have gone around this mountain long enough. Take the bull by the horns, and stand up straight. You have what it takes to lick this devil once and for all. His back has already been crushed by Jesus. Empty your basket of every negative thought and word spoken or written about you. Roll up your sleeves!

Game Plan—Your Move!

If you are game, travel this journey with me as you check out your own licenses. Take and use as many as you need. There's more where they came from—God's warehouse.

The big question now is who is controlling this project? When you know who has called you then you know you are in the right business.

When you hear and heed His voice, your permission to do so comes naturally to you. Your natural instincts, or call it what you will, allow you to go on autopilot most of the time. In most situations you find yourself in, who you are and who you belong to are part of your consciousness. I know in the secret recesses of your mind, you want someone to be driving. Allow Him therefore to be your chauffeur today. He knows all the turns and curves on the roads of life. He also knows where all the irritating bumps are. Do you want what He has? Then *commit* your life to *Him* today. I am sure you feel the tug in your heart. I see that smile forming. Let it rip. You had a million reasons why you turned away.

People let you down. Get over it. You don't have to live with that negative mind-set. I don't want to hear any more excuses. This is the greatest gift you can ever receive. Open your arms wide to collect all you can—all or nothing.

Angels are waiting to welcome you. Let the Master lead you through a victorious living and to a victorious life. Let us journey on together!

CHAPTER 1
Licensed to Adore ... Him

Who is the object of your adoration? I hope you will say that Christ and His love register high on the Richter scale of your emotions. We thrive on relationships. God has wired us that way. But what causes us to fall in love one day and out of love the next? One minute we feel the tingling, warm feeling down our spines. We hope that euphoric phase will last forever. But then life happens. We wake up to bad breath. By the way, you have it too. Bad breath, I mean.

Today, you have the license to adore your loved one—the one who will never disappoint you. He will never manipulate you or condemn you for anything. But to have lasting adoration, you have the license to adore the One who has given you the desire to love – God Almighty. Adore Him today.

As a beginning, let's explore the story of one who adored Him with all she had. Picture her for a minute. She might have come in through the back door. She didn't feel she deserved to be there among the members of the inner circle. She came from the country and didn't belong to the country club. Her clothes didn't fit the environment in which she found herself. She came in regardless. She didn't speak the language of the palace. Still, she forged ahead. She didn't have the code, but she pressed on. She was a woman in a man's world. Nothing stopped her. She felt His irresistible pull. She adored Him. That was the license that gave her access to Him, who can love unconditionally. She watched Him, who is the resurrection and the life. She came in her brokenness. She bowed with confidence before Him. She came into His presence because He knew her heart. He welcomed her into His life. Did she have a degree to her name? I don't think so. She came as she was. The proof of her license was wrapped up in that alabaster jar of expensive, perfumed oil. She didn't hold back. She poured it all on Him, onto His feet. She had the license to adore Him, and she used it.

The one Jesus loved gave back to Him in adoration. With her alabaster jar of oil, she showed us that we can worship Him as we are. Where are you today? Down in the dumps or down with it? Who or what is your alabaster jar? Break him or her at the feet of Jesus today. Give up that addiction. He will give you something more lasting. What is it that you have done in secret for so long? What are you tired of hiding?

I remember when my son and I needed to make a 9-1-1 call to heaven. My son desperately needed to have a license that would give him permission to remain in the United States. For some inexcusable reason, his residency permit had expired. We broke our alabaster jar of oil at the Lord's feet. What did we do? Every evening at 11:00 p.m. for a month, we sang praises to Him for an hour. Have you heard about that mighty move of God during the midnight hour? God performed that miracle for my son because within two weeks, officials at the Immigration and Naturalization Services waived the residency status requirement and gave him a citizenship license. The God I know honors us when we humble ourselves and give Him praise and worship. You actually can try this at home. He is the God of "the nick of time." He will answer today when you call Him. Check out His word in Jeremiah 33:3.

Do you still want the license? What have you got to lose? Don't chicken out now. You have come this far.

Remember—you have the license to adore Him.

Break your alabaster jar and cover Him with praises. When you love Him that much, He will help you to gain entry to the country club of your dreams.

CHAPTER 2
Licensed to Ask ... Him

What can I do for you? The Bible is full of people who have heard the same question. Can you hear the same question now? What can God do for you? How can Holy Spirit help you? Come on, don't be shy. He has heard your heart's cry. He actually knows everything you have ever done and will do. But you do not have because you do not ask.

Thousands of years ago, Solomon heard Him say, "Ask me for anything."

Solomon had the license to ask because he came from a winner's lineage. After all, his father, David, was a man after God's own heart. God wants your heart today!

God gave Solomon more than he expected—the greatest riches in the world and peace in his days. The greatest gift Solomon requested was wisdom. Do you wonder why Solomon was labeled the wisest man who ever lived? God gave him the license to operate in His name. And he used it to the fullest—Solomon enjoyed his life so much that he said degrees and pedigrees are all vanity. Everything on earth is temporal.

Aspire for eternal things like the license you have decided to receive today.

Now, because you have confessed Jesus as your Lord and Savior, you belong to His kingdom. You have a new lineage, a new family. You are armed with the license to ask whatsoever you want, using the only name that every institution around the world recognizes. At this moment, you are credentialed with the license to ask.

What do you want? Be careful what you ask for. Be careful to ask with the right motives. Remember that it is all right to ask for material things. Do you really need that extra pair of athletic shoes? I just counted fifteen in your closet. Put down that blazer. What is your excuse this time? Come on, you have a dozen of the same design.

Ask that your cup be filled with blessings that moth and rust will not destroy.

Ask for joy that will flow like rivers out of your belly.

Ask for peace even in the fiercest storm.

Ask for wisdom that you may make decisions that will honor God.

Ask for a lifestyle that people will see and want what and who you have. Advertise Jesus today as the Author and Finisher of our faith, the hope of glory.

Shout to the world with a loud voice about the goodness of the Lord. You have the license to ask … Him.

Maybe you think that Solomon already had a glowing résumé

coming from a royal lineage. Or you might think that he benefited from living in Old Testament times.

Let's go to the New Testament camp for a short while! A certain man was so sick that his friends decided to open a hole in the roof of a house and lower him through the hole, placing him at the feet of Jesus. .

The long and short of it was that the befriended man met Jesus face-to-face. What have you risked or lost because things were not going right? You can meet Jesus right now. Your approach doesn't have to be as dramatic as cutting through the roof of a house. Let me offer you a friendly warning: following Jesus involves taking risks. I can assure you that the journey will be worth every single waking moment of your life. He already finished the work on the cross so you and I can open up our redemptive package and pull out our license to ask.

Ask for healing for your loved ones today! Ask for God's touch in your lives!

In another New Testament account, Jairus asked for help with his daughter, and Jesus made her whole. Do you know that wherever Jesus went, He was doing great miracles? He still is in the business today. You have the license to *ask* and you shall *receive, seek* and you shall *find, knock* and the door shall be *opened*.

What is that one big need you have today?

I can't count the number of things I have asked God for over the years. But I can surely count my blessings. Honestly, I thank God for all the times He told me *no*. I want to thank Him for the people He brought into my life and the people He weeded out. It hurt then, but now I know all things work together for my good.

Where is that heartthrob you thought would be with you forever? He traded you at forty for two twenties. Ouch! I look back on the day I received my divorce papers. It hurt, you bet. I am not glorifying divorce (because God hates divorce), but I am glad that Jesus happened to me. What if I had still been married and didn't discover His love until later? At His appointed time, He makes all things beautiful. I am blessed beyond measure! I will be glad to let that blessing overflow into your life. That's why you are still reading. Be blessed, dear friend.

Ask Him!

CHAPTER 3
Licensed to Believe ... Him

Your License—Your World

In today's world of technology, what do you believe? You believed in the daily planner binder at one point. Next was the Rolodex (daily planner) that you couldn't wait to show off. Then came the PDA (daily planner), and now God help us, then came the FILO fax (daily planner). Now we walk around touting the Blackberry, the smartphones, the "i" this and "i" that. It's a never-ending display of new and newer gadgets. You cannot keep up with ever-evolving technology, soon to become the world's primary language.

We cannot but marvel at the power God has given humanity to make all of these comforts available to us. You know, of course, that He wants to give you the power to make wealth.

Remember—if you are hooked on drugs today, there is help around the corner.

Your dependence on alcohol can only numb the pain for a season.

Your body is precious to Holy Spirit. He wants to abide in you.

Why will you not let Him in today? He desires to fill that void in you that nothing and no one else can fill.

The loneliness will pale in comparison. The in-dwelling power of Holy Spirit in you will give you a permanent high. The gang family will leave you in time, either through death, accidents, or a change of heart. What is your family going to do without your support? Leave that footloose and fancy-free woman alone. She has only come to entice you for a reason and a season—to steal from you. When the money runs out, she will run to the next available sucker. You are a winner! Believe God for yourself!

CHAPTER 4
His License

You have the license to be a winner and you want to throw that all away? Yes, you can throw the garbage out on a regular basis, but God is God. He still allows U-turns! Make one right now because He is waiting. I can see Jesus talking to God on your behalf.

Remember that He can drive you. He knew you didn't have the foggiest idea how to get out of that hole you dug for yourself. He has a smile on His face. He will not condemn you. All He wants and will say to you is welcome back. Did you hear about Ray-Ray, the Philanderer? He came home, you know. You wonder why his wife of twenty-five years received him with open arms and tenderly looked into his eyes and saw the remorse and pain he went through. She already retrieved her license from the dust-filled box hidden in the closet. She picked up her Bible once more. She chose to use her God-given rights to fight for her family. She dared to believe *Him*.

It seems like yesterday. Right now I may look like I'm battle weary, but I still have some fight left in me, more than I think. I have fought for my family—that is, my son. One time he ran away from home. The heat was too much in the kitchen. I challenged him to live a life worthy of the license he carries. I thank God for the legacy I have in Christ Jesus. You have heard of tough love. I applied it in the crudest form—changed the locks and kept smiling. He came to church as usual, found time to say hello, and then bounced back to the streets. I kept my faith and kept on smiling and praying. Today I am happy to announce that he is married, with a family that sings and praises God all the time. God will come through for you too, my dear. Dare to believe Him who promised that you and your children are for signs and wonder for the glory of God. Check out what Isaiah wrote in 8:18:

"Behold, I and the children whom the LORD hath given me are for signs and for wonders in Israel from the LORD of hosts."

We still have a family, a body of Christ that prays for unseen faces too. Your beliefs are embedded in who you are and who you will become. Now to live an overcoming life, you must have the license to believe.

You believe that when you brandish that passport and visa to go to any foreign country, the airline, customs, the country have given you the permission to move freely around. By the way, the visa only allows you entry for as long as is stipulated on your document. You believe you can take that vacation of your dreams.

Believe *Him*!

I read about this guy named Zaccheus who knew he needed such a license, an entry. He heard that Jesus was passing by but couldn't compete with the crowd.

You see, not only was he short, he was also a tax collector, a hated man. What is your handicap, or what do you think is your shortcoming? You can overcome that today.

Zaccheus struck while the iron was hot and hit the jackpot. Being short in stature, he chose to climb a sycamore tree so he could catch a glance of this Jesus everyone was raving about. Jesus this and Jesus that! Enough already! He too had to see this popular rock star Jesus whom everyone flocked to see. Mind you, he believed.

All he needed was proof. His belief caused him to defy everything and everyone and pledge to give back to anyone he ever swindled or cheated. His reward came in a big way. Something great happened to him—something great that money cannot buy. It affected others around him too. Jesus wants to give you the license today. He has extended it to you.

Accept it—*salvation*.

"And Jesus said to him, 'Today salvation has come to this house, because he, too, is a son of Abraham.'" You must believe that you are the seed of Abraham and so you have the free license to the one who can save you from: addiction, inordinate affections, drugs, gangs, prostitution, pornography, pain, disease, small sin, big sin, sins of omission, sins of commission, generational curses, adultery, and tax collectors.

His License

There is no name mentioned that can be higher than the name of Jesus. Every knee must bow, and every tongue must confess that Jesus is Lord. Now you have your license to believe *Him*. What do you have to lose anyway? Has it worked out the way you planned it? Then give this a chance. There you go—receive your license now! Are you hesitating? Call His name and He will answer. Go ahead! *Jesus*!

CHAPTER 5
Licensed to Dance ...
for Him and ... with Him

I used to think that Christian life was boring. Am I the only one who ever had those thoughts and doubts? You see, I love to dance and party. I thought I would miss all the parties and shindigs if I took the license from God. Contrary to popular belief, Christianity is one conscious effort to have fun. When I watched Christian movies about Jesus, I used to marvel that every producer/director shows Him as having fun, always smiling. Except of course when He died on the cross for our sins, which was painful. You must purpose in your heart that this is a rich journey full of ups and downs. Needless to say, I am having a ball. Life is so much sweeter today than I ever thought. Guess what? I am not in this alone. That's why I have written this book, so you and I can enjoy this wonderful Jesus together. His love is contagious, you know. You feel it too, don't you?

Jesus is my dancing partner, and He is a smooth operator. All I did was first hear the music. You have to hear this. I bought a house

13

nineteen years ago, and I thought to have a housewarming party for friends and family. I remember the music we listened and danced to all night was a song titled, "Send Me, Jesus." I even had it on auto repeat on my long commute to work. You could catch me bobbing my head to the music. He took my word for it—God became my lifelong designated dancing partner. He has never stepped on my dainty toes. My life has never been the same. He sure sent me. I never thought it was possible to have this kind of joy. Don't think for a minute that I don't go through. I don't live in la-la land (anymore).

As a middle school teacher of two decades, you know we have more than "bad hair days." We have challenges with a capital C. I take all in my stride by letting He who is leading to make me a leader over the situations that come against me.

As a matter of fact, most mornings, I hear His music playing. What a jovial God, tickling my ears with melodies to usher me into His presence. I trust Him to lead accurately without fear of Him stepping on my toes. He loves to dance with me too. Most times, I don't even need fancy clothes or evening gowns. He can dance with me anytime He chooses, and whenever He plays; He is my melody and harmony.

He is my morning song; He is my evening song.

His symphony is far greater than Beethoven, Mozart, and the great composers of the centuries.

Sing to Him with a joyful voice today. Don't worry that you can't carry a tune. Never mind because He is singing through you anyway. Is that a tuxedo you want to don? Do you want to put on that ball gown? It doesn't matter to Him. Come as you are—bring yourself and your appetite. He has invited you and me to this elegant feast prepared by the Master Chef Himself. What an honor. He has pulled out all the stops, with the best linens and finest china fit for royalty. You are from a royal lineage.

Did you catch Him the other day at the party in Canaan? He was having such a blast that His friends and family wondered. They thought He was going to be a party pooper. But His mom knew what He could do. She knew her Son, the Messiah, was one great bartender. Imagine turning water into wine. The guests were dumbfounded. Why did He wait this long to show Himself? Ask Him yourself.

I ask myself sometimes what I did to deserve a first dance. You remember your last prom? You still have the pictures to show how much fun you had. After your prom, did you have a reason to end up with a license not to dance with the student voted to be the most likely to be a famous astronaut, but with a license to dance with … Him? Here is the deal.

His License

This is one party that He has already saved the first dance for you. He also has saved the last dance for you in case you missed His first invitation. He is not mad at you—you didn't RSVP. He has forgiven your faux pas. You now have the social graces to allow you entry; you have the license to dance with Him. He has extended His hand of grace to you. Place your hand gently in His. Let Him lead you.

Where is the party tonight? Can Jesus be invited to the next party you will have? Pop the champagne! It's celebration time.

Why did He change my water into wine? I am the apple of His eye because He first loved me. He chose me according to His word in Matthew 15. I just placed my hands in His and He leads.

He waits. You can now use the license you have to dance for *Him* and with *Him*. Can you hear the music in your car as you commute? Is it a slow dance or the salsa? Foxtrot, Harlem shake, hen, or chicken dance. He is down with it!

Dear competitor, you are the next champion on *Dancing with the Stars*. Your next video footage is ready to be shot. You have the best choreographers to appear on your next video. Allow me to be the first to congratulate you on your number one spot. I see you bobbing your head to His music. He has the full orchestra, synchronized, in one accord, serenading you.

You got the moves, dance with … *Him.*

You got your dancing shoes on, dance with … *Him.*

You got the clothes, you look the part, dance with … *Him.*

The disco lights are shining brightly on you; dance with … *Him.*

Here is your license.

Take one step forward and then another; just keep dancing with … *Him.*

CHAPTER 6
Licensed to Eat ... with Him

Put that fork down! Bow your head and give thanks. It won't make the food disappear. Listen, who gave you the food on that table? The fine linen, china, and silverware that are beautifully displayed came from somewhere. Yes, you guessed right! You are grateful for all He has and will continue to provide.

Ask the little boy with his sack lunch. Imagine him clutching his lunch bag to his chest after a long morning. His eyes look beyond what is going on around him. He can smell the fish and can't wait to open his bag, pull out his lunch, and dig in. He thought of how his mom had lovingly prepared this special lunch for him. Yummy! "*No*! You mean He wants my lunch. I wish I had eaten it when I had the chance. The one called Andrew, one of the disciples of Jesus., wants my lunch. No way!" This young lad became a celebrity because he gave. From the minute he looked longingly at his lunch, rummaged in his knapsack for the little bread and fish, and handed it over—one minute. You guessed it. He has his sixty seconds of fame. A lunch that was meant for one person managed to feed—guess what? One little boy's lunch fed five thousand people! Have you ever wondered how proud this young lad must have felt? I bet the people around him will have been green with envy, wishing they had been the one. The young lad too might have felt and walked like he was ten feet tall. We serve a miracle-working God!

You are a celebrity in the making. What is on your lunch menu? You hold riches and treasures in your hand that could feed a million people.

You have the license to eat ... with *Him*. You might have only a dollar to your name, but He is ready if you will invest in Him. Allow Him to use what He has placed in your hands to do big exploits for Him. Wash up, and put on your finest outfit; you have been summoned to dine with Him. Do you know how to use your fork and knife when you are in an elegant setting? I wasn't sophisticated enough to know which piece of the cutlery to use first. He will teach you how to sit elegantly at table (no slouching), drink your soup without slurping, and eat the main course with the right utensils and the right conversation, with the right people. God knows the friends you should spend your time with, make small talk with, and brush aside. You have business to take care of. Thank You, Jesus. Take the first bite.

You have the license to eat ... yes, your vegetables. I know you are like me, tired of researchers coming up with different findings. Eat this and not that! Even the labels lie if you are not a careful reader. You and I are not illiterates. Read and understand what your food is telling you. God made the grains and wheat. You have the license today to eat all you can; just the right stuff. Deal? Start by being conscious of what you have in your hand. And ... exercise. Don't let me over stress the point. You don't need a membership card at a gym to work out—all you need is your license to eat with Him. He will guide your taste buds, make you like the things that are good for you, make you change your lifestyle all for Him. Listen to your body. Do you have a deal?

PS: Please know that you can go to the gym if that is your thing. It just doesn't work for me. I am a park exercise kind of person.

CHAPTER 7
Licensed to Think ... Like Him

How did Nelson Mandela survive in prison for twenty years? Do you ever wonder the kids of thoughts that went through his mind, year after year? From prison to the palace! We all like to read such "and they all lived happily ever after" stories. We choose to forget the "in betweens." Everyone wakes up with bad breath.

Personally, there are many thoughts I wish I could obliterate, or expunge. One of my favorite maxims is: "Change your thoughts and you change your world."

What are your thoughts right now? Thoughts like what you are going to wear to the party or school or job. Thoughts like:

- your future ... and all it entails
- your family ... and all their idiosyncrasies
- your job ... and promotions and unfairness
- your world
- the society
- your goals

- your ambitions
- your pleasures—food, music, family harmony

Did you ever hear about the man named Elijah? He was an ordinary man like you and me. Yet he used his license to the fullest advantage. He thought like God did. He mocked those who were worshiping idols. He dared their gods to show up. However, when Elijah spoke to his God, He answered him by fire. It gets better. When Elijah went up to heaven, he gave Elisha, his protégé, his mantle. But you see, Elisha followed him around because he liked the way Elijah thought. One of the miracles Elisha did that strikes a chord in me is when a borrowed ax fell into the river, Elisha simply pulled it out. Or did you read about his escapades with a Shunammite woman? He prayed for her, God answered and gave the woman a son. Later on, the boy died. Instead of fretting and weeping, the woman simply went back to Elisha and asked him some poignant questions. To make a long story short, the miracle she thought was dead came back to life. We echo her words by praying, "It shall be well with me." What kind of thought went through his mind? Did he have doubts, or did he simply think, *If I saw my mentor do such exploits, then I too can do the same*? And you see, Elisha had his double share of the anointing that was on Elijah.

Both men had licenses to think like God did.

Nelson Mandela did. I have changed my thinking drastically.

I now have a kingdom mind-set.

What about you?

Ask God to breathe on the miracles you thought were dead. It is resurrection time!

Today, I challenge you to think like Jesus does. That miracle is still applicable to our lives. Prophesy to your life that whatever miracles God will use you for, right now, you have the license to think like He does. You have the kingdom mind-set—use your license to dream big. Use your license to think good and pure thoughts.

Something good will happen to you today.
Decisions that you will make will honor God.
It shall be well with you.
What is your next move?
Your dead miracle will come back to life.
Use your license to think like *Him*.

I used to go through life like I was in la-la land. I thought everybody should like me. I used to think I didn't want to be rich. I used to think I existed just for me and my immediate family. I even went through the nine months of pregnancy in a constant state of euphoria. And then labor pains hit my lower back. Needless to say, childbirth is a miracle on its own. To our miracle God, You alone could have thought of this eye-popping, teeth-gnashing, and unforgettable experience.

It was usually every man for himself and God for us all. Wherever that quote came from, that's not what God says. That's a selfish mind-set and not in God's agenda. I had this myopic picture of the world. May God deliver us from mediocre living and thinking!

Then Jesus happened! When I knew I had a license, a bracelet with my name blinking like neon signs, I carry it with pride. Nothing can stand in my way. I know that I should have blessings in abundance so I can be a blessing to others.

Enemies will come by way of the following:

- small voices telling you that you are wasting your time, believing in God, Jesus, and Holy Spirit.
- disappointments
- diseases and deaths
- prodigal children
- love the riches of the world
- prioritize me
- setbacks

But I have news for you—they all pale in comparison to what you can enjoy when you have His license to think like *Him*.

You see, I know that my victory has been bought. I have my license, and it's stamped with the blood of Jesus. No demon in hell can stop my God-given license to prosper. I have been appointed for greatness. You too have the license today. Are you wearing yours, or have you hidden it? My beloved, there is nothing more fulfilling than to know you are now thinking like Him. God has a divine purpose for you. Let the game begin! Move your pieces from small to big.

Move your chips from low to high.

Move your tiles from mediocre to grand.

Move your cards from prison to palace.

Move your name from corporal to general.

Move your ball into the court.

Yes, your closets may be full of hand-me-downs today, second-hand clothes yesterday. But when you start thinking like Jesus does, you will see yourself clothed in designer outfits before you actually wear them. Joseph thought like that too. He dressed up when his turn came to be presented before Pharaoh. He shed the ragged clothes of his prison days and put on royal garments that allowed him entrance to the palace. The rest is history. Read more about him in the Bible (book of Exodus).

CHAPTER 8
Licensed to Change ... for Him

Change your clothes.
Change your hair.
Change your beds.
Change your friends.
Change your habits.
Change your thinking.
Change! Change! Change!

Ten years from now, will these matter? Check out your prom pictures if you can find them. Better still, next time you go to your high school reunion, see your eyes lock with your high school sweetheart whom you haven't seen in twenty-five years. He is still dating "poly" and "ester." You now wonder what you ever saw in him. Take it from me—even one year from now, what or who you thought meant the whole world to you might not be part of your life anymore. Everything is temporal. Change happens to all. The buzzword in our world today is *change*. Society is capitalizing on it. Change is actually not new to God. Life happens. Solomon—remember him—coined it accurately where he said:

> There is an appointed time for everything and there is a time for every event under heaven—A time to give birth and a time to die; A time to plant and a time to uproot what is planted. A time to kill and a time to heal; A time to tear down and a time to build up. A time to weep and a time to laugh; A time to mourn and a time to dance. A time to throw stones and a time to gather stones; A time to embrace and a time to shun embracing. A time to search and a time to give up as lost; A time to keep and a time to throw away. A time to tear apart and a time to sew together; A time to be silent and a time to speak. A time to love and a time to hate; A time for war and a time for peace.

Do these nuggets of truth resonate in your spirit? Like a well-known commercial asks, "Are you in good hands?" You are if you hand everything to Jesus. You are ready for change when you know that nothing matters but your soul. God made you and said you are good. That means He made you, you arrogant one. You can't even make the yeast that makes the bread you eat. Yet, you want to boast in your accomplishments. Yes, you are a straight-A student; you have all the trophies to show your athletic abilities; you are a wonderful wife and mother. Better start boasting in the one who put those goodies in you. You are who God says you are—born to win and destined to prosper. You have the license to change—you.

Wait a minute. You mean I can wear whatever I want? I will turn the question back to you. Be honest and ask yourself—can I invite Him into my heart when my pants are worn down so low that my underwear is showing? Or what if your breasts are popping out of their encasement? That's clearly a premeditated wardrobe malfunction. It is time for damage control here. Change your thinking and you change your world. You have the license to change … for *Him*. Wear your name tag, dog tag, tattoo, um, your license with pride. You have earned it. This license is better than a PhD. He gave it to you, His special friend. Look at the new you! You have a new picture on your license now. Enjoy your freedom.

CHAPTER 9
Licensed to Speak ... for Him

Do you have something to say? You have a voice, don't you? Do you remember the last time you said you couldn't catch a break? It seemed like everything you did turned to mush. Any time you opened your mouth, your words didn't make sense even to you. Now it's time to speak for *Him*. Kind of reminds me of a beauty pageant competitor who stumbled at all her sentences. You would think with all her grooming, she would have it all together. But she didn't.

It's time to speak for *Him*. Now it is time to open your mouth. You have enough in you to make sense. You have the license to speak for *Him*.

Forget the intrusions in your thoughts, the unfounded rumors about you, and the last time you stood up on stage and froze with fright.

You are not alone. Remember Moses, the deliverer? He had a speech impediment like you do. God didn't let his excuses stop him from achieving His divine purpose for Moses. You see how God tricked him? After his complaints and all, God allowed him to use

Aaron, his brother, as a crutch. But God always has the last say. After all his huffing and puffing, God promised that Aaron would be his mouthpiece. Isn't it just like our God to turn the tables on us? Moses ended up speaking to Pharaoh on behalf of God.

God gave him a license to speak for ... *Him.*

Stand on the mountaintop today and speak for ... *Him.*

You are standing on a gold mine in your home, in your school, on your job, on the airplane, in the mall, in the PTO meetings, at the bus stop, at church, in the hospital, and at the next New Year's party.

Wherever the soles of your feet have touched, you have the license to speak for ... *Him.*

CHAPTER 10
Licensed to Sing ... for Him

You have a record deal signed up already. You have the license today. You don't need to sign a contract. You know those contracts are not worth their weight in gold. That partnership turned sour, and you are scared of trying again. The other party decided to renege on the deal when you couldn't deliver what you promised.

Here is a deal from the one who has signed that license for you, no strings attached. Are you game? Quit strumming your fingers on the dining room table. It's time to bring out the tambourine. Get your praise shoes on. It's show time. Who is number one on your fan club list? Is your mom rooting for you? Trust me, God placed her there. Is your dad at every ball game? Believe me, God placed the desire in him. Never mind that he embarrasses you sometimes with the yells when you score and then yells at the referee for a bad call. God wired him that way. You see, God Himself cannot physically be present at your recitals and sports events. But He is your greatest fan. He has a lot invested in you, more than your trust fund, even more than your college funds. He has a license that has your name on it—you are the best kept secret in town waiting to be signed up by the biggest record label. Do you have your dream team? The angels in heaven wait to join you in chorus. Sing, sister; sing it, brother! Accept your deal and receive your license from the one who has anointed your voice to *sing* … for *Him*.

Now you have the next footage for your video—your license copied into the biggest gathering of stars. You are at the top. Move over, Aretha. Are you ready for your photo shoot for your next album? It's already a hit, you know. I confess that I got a sneak peek at the nominations. Your name seems to pop up because you are highly favored of the Lord. Way to go!

Here is your long-awaited moment—you can now *sing* … for *Him*.

CHAPTER 11
Licensed to Pray ... to Him

You got milk? Imagine your T-shirt emblazoned with the words, *you got prayer*!

Who are those in the Hall of Faith who prayed? You are on the A-list. My name is there too. You see, your prayer has been answered. There is more where that came from—more answers from heaven. Pray without ceasing because the prayer of the righteous goes a long way. One of my prayer points was to be happy. God has done more than I can ever hope for. He injected and infested me with *joy*. With the different challenges we grow through, the devil can't steal my joy. It comes out of me not only in songs and praises, but I have love for my fellow brothers and sisters. Hence this book is a token of the kind of joy God placed in me. In every situation I face, I can take a praise break and shout, "Jesus is *Lord*!" This dependence did not happen in one day. I learned to daily trust Him in little and big things. He always comes through. Join hands with me in prayer because God honors prayers of agreement. What do you need prayer for right now? I lift up that need to the one who can turn the tide in our favor.

If you tell me you do not know to pray, stop. Do you have conversations with your friends, family members, and even strangers? Then you can have a conversation with God. Another excuse—you cannot see Him. He is right there beside you. Simply then, just say the Lord's Prayer (New Living Translation):

> Pray like this: Our Father in heaven, may your name be kept holy. May Your kingdom come soon. May Your will be done on earth, As it is in heaven. Give us today the food we need, And forgive us our sins, As we have forgiven those who sin against us. And don't let us yield to temptation, But rescue us from the evil one.

You can repeat this prayer as often as you want.
Glory be to God in the highest, for He has heard you.

CHAPTER 12
Licensed to Have Peace ... in Him

You soak in your bathtub, aromatic candles filling the room, and you think you can escape into the temporal peace that provides. Wait till you hear what is in store for you.

I used to travel around with this baggage called worry. Until I met the Prince of Peace, my life was one huge lie. I smiled at the right times, using the correct lingo and all. Little did I know that when God's peace fills you, you have told worry that you are the master over it. You need the peace of Him who has your license in His hand. Right now He has extended it to you. Will you accept it? You can relax in the knowledge that God is supreme, and He is sovereign. Take Him at His word when Jesus said, "Peace I leave with you, my peace I give you" (John 14:27).

How did you go to bed last night? He promised to tuck you in every night. All the herbal tea and drinks put you to bed, but only

God can wake you up from that restful sleep. Appreciate Him, for He alone can perform and give you that gift of life

Remember how Jesus slept while a huge storm raged. Now He is seated on the right hand of God and wants to carry all your burdens so you can sleep like a baby.

Do you remember Daniel who God made to use lions as pillows? He slept well even in the midst of danger. Ask God to visit your subconscious and take out all the noise and distractions, lies from the enemy, and ask for His peace that nobody can understand.

Ask Him for His peace, and know that this is the day He made. You will rejoice and be glad. Go to sleep, beloved, because He has promised to give you rest.

CHAPTER 13
Licensed to Write ... to Him

This manual came about as a result of obedience. Growing up, the first thing I wanted to be was a journalist, then an advertising executive with an ocean-view office. For years I had jingles ringing in my head. Little did I know that today I got my wish, all right. I now advertise Jesus the way He wants. I journal to Him every day, and I love it. There is such a relief knowing that He knows what I will write about before I do. It's great to know that He actually reads my mail. It tickles me when my pastor talks about something I am going through. I shake my head and say, "Lord, once more You read my e-mail to him."

I thank God every day for all you out there with a license to write. I pray that many more will see the benefits of writing. You have the license to write ... to *Him*. Your book may not be a bestseller; write anyway. You need to make a withdrawal from your account. What account? The one He set up for you when you accepted Him as *Lord* and *Savior*.

CHAPTER 14
Licensed to Write ... for Him

Scratch that. Delete that. Look at the gospels of the Bible, Matthew, Mark, Luke, and John wrote. They were ordinary people like you and me. Let's start with Matthew, a tax collector. In his days, he was despised by the people because of the nature of his job. Yet, he was a disciple of Jesus and wrote about Jesus to the Jews, the Messiah King of all kings. Next time you visit your CPA, and imagine how unlikely he could be to be one of the contributors to your bestseller novel. Do not trivialize all that God has placed in you. Mark, the other writer, was not a disciple of Jesus. But he too wrote about the teachings of Jesus, showing how Jesus came not to be served but to serve, a Servant Messiah. You can be a leader and still be a servant. Follow the example of Jesus and understand that:

> "And hast made us unto our God kings and priests:
> and we shall reign on the earth" (Revelation 5:10).

A doctor by profession, Luke also has a place in history, a purpose for his existence. He had the honor to write an accurate account of the life of Jesus as Deliverer Messiah.

Last but not the least, John, the Son of Thunder, an apostle, wrote that Jesus is the Son of God, God in the flesh. We have eternal life when we believe in Him.

Do you believe that these writers were inspired by the Holy Ghost? Jesus is who He said He is. He walked on water, you know. He spoke the word two thousand years ago, and His word has the power to move mountains out of your way today. There is power in the blood of Jesus. You can have that power today because like Father like son, you belong to Him. Who is your audience? Whom can you write to about *Him*? What can you write about *Him*? Do like I did. I first had to know *Him*. I used to joke to my high school Sunday school classes as I worked them through the different stages of knowing Jesus for themselves. I used the analogy of the secular way of knowing in a boy/girl relatable way. First is the knowing stage. You exchange phone numbers and all. Then you gingerly enter the text messaging stage. You get bolder, flirting with him, throwing hints here and there. You like him, he likes you. This stage is fraught with frustrations from both parties. You want him to ask for more, but you are not willing to give him. You want the future to be right now. Not only have you started the wedding plans, you have also named your children and the private schools, colleges, and careers your children will have.

You want so much, but caution makes you tread softly. What if … he is the one or not the one? Are we going to have ten children or one? Is our house going to be bigger and nicer than the Joneses'? Are we going to vacation in Hawaii every spring? How much are you really saying in the relationship? How much are you not saying in this relationship? You are happy and elated one minute, and the next you want to call it quits. You are tired of the roller coaster rides. Why do you have these queasy feelings in the pit of your stomach and you are not pregnant? It's all part of the process. Now the relationship is stabilizing.

Yes, the late-night phone calls. You eagerly wait for his calls where he whispers sweet nothings in your ears. He just has to hear your voice one last time before he goes to bed.

You can tell he is in love with you, and the feeling is reciprocated. But wait a minute now. This relationship is going way too fast for you. You want him to slow down because you are thinking about him all the time. You want to spend all of your waking moments at his side. He waits—he is the hunter, after all, with all natural male instincts in full gear. You are in. The die is cast, sold, hook, line, and sinker. Your mind is no longer yours. Now, after a whirlwind romance, you still can't find your feet, let alone see your toes, and he bends on one knee and pops the question. Will you marry me? You thought the question would never come, didn't you? He was biding his time all along. He knew you came from a royal priesthood from day one.

He saw how you acted around strangers, family, friends, siblings, neighbors, and classmates.

He saw how you:

- cried with compassion when your pet hamster died
- rejoiced over your friend's promotion when you didn't get what you clearly deserved
- lamented over the injustice done to the homeless shelter
- signed up first to serve at the soup kitchen.

He saw how you dressed up for:

- a trip to the mall
- a trip to the movies
- an outing with your family
- a date with him

You were consistent.

He watched you:

- sing to a sick baby at the hospital
- read to the folks at the old people's home
- cook for the potluck dinner for the exchange students from around the world
- choose a road less traveled by getting a C instead of an A where your friends saw the answers to the finals.

You came prequalified because you were predestined by God before you were formed in your mother's womb.

Now you understand why you were chosen to carry the license to write for … *Him.*

You have what it takes. It's already in you. Your DNA is *His.* He bought you, remember?

Now you are wearing His ring, married to Him. Show off your "bling" to the world! You love the attention and spotlight, don't you? Now you see how you can write for … *Him.* You have testimonies yet untold. Bring out your journal right now. Write about:

- your day, the ups and downs,
- your goals and how God can help fulfill them
- your family and their support
- your job and the challenges.
- the latest diagnosis from the doctor
- whom you want to date or marry
- your desire to move to another state or follow that dream.
- your dreams and your purpose on earth.

You have a lot to say, don't you? Promise me that you will just write. When anything comes to you, just pen it down. I bet you an exhilarating feeling that no one but God can fill you with. You have your bestseller inside of you, waiting to be tapped. Don't wait any longer for your license to write for … He is with you.

CHAPTER 15
Licensed to Grow ... in Him

Please tell me why it is necessary to have a shave – beard, legs and whatever you need to remove. It will grow back, you know. It's time to invest in something that will grow and become a harvest. Seriously, you have a license to make you grow in Him. First, you know you have what it takes. You have in you a treasure or a seed that is just waiting to be released. Put that seed in the ground and watch it grow. What is your seed?

A talent—use it.
A gift—unwrap it.
An idea—write it down.
A vision—write it.
A job—work it.
A testimony—share it.
A dream—promote it.
A family—nurture it.
A game—play it.

A vacation—enjoy it.

What do all these have in common? They all grow or have the potential for growth. But what does it take to make your dream grow, for example? Look the part and there is no charge. Let's keep it real. Let's get you on the growth train. Get ready for the ride of your life.

Put it in the ground—by faith.

Water it by faith and season it with love.

God will cause you to have the increase. Trust Him that He is more than able.

In addition, you may want to read Matthew 13, which is full of parables about seed, the sower, and what the enemy can do to any unsuspecting person. You want your seed to fall on good soil, where it will produce a crop—a hundred, sixty, or thirty times what you sowed (Matthew 13:8).

Faith without action is dead. Put on your brand new farmer's overalls, boots, and shovel and get to digging. Your Father has guaranteed you a bountiful harvest.

Grow ... in Him.

CHAPTER 16
Licensed to Love ... Him

When was the last time you did something nice for someone? I just remember the song, "What have you done for me lately?" Whether it is the remix or the old jive, God is asking what you have done for someone to bring a smile to his or her lips or eyes. Did your eyes just mist over because you knew you could have but you didn't? Don't fret. It's all good. I know that is grammatically incorrect, but you get my point. Times are tough, and you can hardly do this or afford that.

The greatest command given to man is to love his neighbor as himself. How do you love God whom you haven't seen? Love your neighbor. I wish it were that simple. There is a plethora of reasons why you can't surely love another. Hey, don't look at me. Ask Him who commanded because He knows.

He knows:

- You can love an adopted child because you can't have yours biologically.

- You can love a strong-willed child who challenges your every kind gesture.
- You can love an adulterous spouse.
- You can love one who raped you.
- You can love one who murdered your only child.
- You can love a back stabber.
- You can love one who turned you away when it was freezing cold and you became homeless.
- You can love a brother who told you that you were not worth fighting for.

This is not a place for levity. This love business is serious. God did it and does it all the time. He sent His only Son so He could take away the sin of the world. He wants to pour His love on you. Perhaps you have no recollection of a father's love. So how do you know that God's love is real? You know what they say. To get love, you have to first give love. Don't waste the rest of your life finding love in the wrong places. This Jesus love is worth finding and keeping. Do you want it? First, I want you to love yourself. Pamper yourself. There are many things to do to take care of you. I have some suggestions for you at the end of this manual. Let's get back to the subject at hand.

I have a story to tell you. Here are two sisters and a brother. All of them loved one man dearly. They had their own way of showing their love. One loved by serving and catering to the physical needs of her family and friends. The other simply loved by gleaning, learning, and soaking in as much knowledge of Him as she could. Then one day, their brother died. You guessed it! This is the story of Mary, Martha, and Lazarus. Needless to say, because of the love shared between these people, Jesus raised Lazarus up from the dead. You see what Jesus did then and many other random acts of kindness, as we want to call them, you too can do today. Ask Him to love that spouse or unloving, rebellious child through you. He will answer because He has given you the license to *love … Him.*

CHAPTER 17
Licensed to Dream ... in Him

What do you see first thing when you wake up? Is it a dream that leaves you going, "No way"? You can't see yourself out of the prison and in a palace, can you? You have the license to dream ... in Him. It's okay to have big dreams. How many "pillow talks" have you had with Joseph, the one with the coat of many colors? Draw comfort from his story. The bigger the dream, the more you know it's beyond your natural or physical capability. The one who is the great I Am has a license with your name on it. Do you want it? Then it is yours. What can you do to earn a residence permit in your palace? All you need is a license from He who owns everything. You see all the oil in the world? He owns all the oil in the ground in every country. What can you do to get some elbow grease? You don't need to do that much. Here, give me your hand. You have the license to dream. Dream *big*! Dream of things your testimony will make people say that there's no way you could have done it on your own. What is your dream?

A multicar garage house ... to raise your family. Remember that with a big house, there will be a big mortgage.

A bestseller book—say it loud!

A Porsche—you have to maintain it too.

A better job—looking good.

A good-looking spouse—the best thing that happened to you, after Jesus.

Joseph dared to dream *big*. He ended up in the palace. He, through no fault of his, ended up in a pit, sold as a slave, and then thrown in prison when he thought surely he had it made. But God still had to process him in the oven some more. He endured till he saw his dreams realized. Only the best is good for you and me because Joseph ended up in the palace, where he became second-in-command to Pharaoh.

Be ready to dream big because we have a *big* God.

Be ready with the answer of why you exist

Be ready to speak about God's faithfulness in making your dream come alive.

Be ready to have a ready answer when called to defend your faith.

Be ready to show your license to *dream* ... in *Him*.

CHAPTER 18
Licensed to Give ... Him

Don't you wish we all had more than the allotted twenty-four hours in a day? What can we do differently than what you are doing right now? What do you need more time for anyway? Perhaps you need more time to:

- sleep in
- start that book project
- go to school
- for your career
- to run errands
- to watch TV
- to shop
- to read a book
- to study
- to meditate
- to pray
- to raise your kids

- to pay off the mortgage
- to pay off the college loan
- to spend quality time with family
- to finish that book
- to cook
- to enjoy that one scoop of ice cream
- to play in the sand
- to look at the moonlight
- to watch the sunset

In everything we do, God wants the service to be dedicated to Him first. You have to first give honor to Him whom honor is due. You have to first know that He is the owner of your:

- body
- life
- time
- family
- job
- loans
- children
- grandchildren
- home
- thoughts
- plans
- visions
- dreams
- ambitions
- money

What then can you offer *Him* today that He didn't already provide? He wants to give you the license to give back to *Him* all that He has given you. I know it sounds confusing. Hey, my God is not an Author of confusion. He just likes spending time with you so you can become well marinated before He puts you in the oven to bake. You want to come out well done, don't you? *Shhhh!* It's a process. He gives and wants you to give back. Not to Him per se but to service unto *Him*.

So think about how you can enrich somebody else's life with your time.

Can you read a book to the elderly, serve as a volunteer in your Sunday school ministry, or become a mentor to a group of teenagers in your neighborhood?

The list goes on of what you can do to *Give ... to Him.*

How much money do you make? I know that question is considered inappropriate, but this is between us. Right! Nobody is here, so you can answer. How much of your take-home pay do you save? I don't want the excuse that you gave last month. When you call it a savings deposit, it is exactly that. Don't dip into it when you need your nails done. Keep your hands out of the till. But I know it's yours. Didn't you tell me that you were saving that for that cool vacation you promised your family three years ago? You need a break, so take it.

CHAPTER 19
Licensed to Touch ... Him

You must have heard of the woman with the issue of blood for twelve years. After all her years of seeking and searching, she touched *Him* in just one defining moment. She followed Him from a distance, watching and waiting for an opportunity to touch. She was driven by one thing only—her faith. The blood that leaked out of her stopped its flow when she touched the hem of His garment.

Whatever it is you have struggled with, in health, finances, or anything that has a name to it (the name of Jesus is higher), just reach out today and touch Him. He is closer than you think.

I recall one particular situation I found myself in. I knew I had to stretch my faith like a rubber ball. A couple of years earlier, my son needed heart surgery. He had been a perfectly healthy boy, playing tournaments all over the region in All-Star games. He discovered that he had irregular heartbeats, and so the doctors chose surgery. We prayed and knew my son would come out okay, by the healing blood of Jesus.

On the day of the surgery, I went boldly to the waiting room with all our family members in attendance. We all gather like that for emergencies and celebrations. I for one was prayed up. Hey, that's my son you are talking about!

Anyway, before my son was wheeled in for prep and all, the surgeon and his nurse came out for introductions. I had prayed that God would give me an opportunity to touch the attending physicians. Needless to say, I released God's anointing already on me into the surgeon and nurse's hands. I felt a release and knew this case was a done deal to the glory of God. The surgeon promised that the surgery would last an hour and tried to explain that it was a routine procedure to him.

He didn't bargain on the devil trying to sabotage God's purpose. We have to fight back because the weapons of our warfare are not carnal but are mighty through God to the pulling down of strongholds.

After seven grueling hours, he came out saying he had actually earned his money. You might be wondering what we felt and how we reacted during those long hours. I have to confess that I didn't eat at that time. I continued praying, called an out-of-state friend to give her an update, and continued praying.

All I knew was I have touched *Him*, my God, my Father, who will not allow us eat the bread of sorrow. I praise Him. I knew I had to touch that surgeon that day before he operated on my son.

I can testify today, twelve years later, that my son is the healthiest young man I have ever seen. To God be all the glory.

I can recommend this formula to you. Find every opportunity to touch Him right now. Believe Him for the healing of your body, finances, family members, you name it.

Above all, you have the authority in the name of *Jesus* to touch the hem of His garment. He is waiting for you to reach out to *Him* today. Stretch out your hand and place it in His. His hand is mighty to save, deliver, provide, protect, hide you, catch you, take you there (wherever your "there" is), go that extra mile, and leap over walls.

Trust God today!

CHAPTER 20
Licensed to Talk to ... Him!

Run to the throne today and not the phone. Nobody can accuse you of being insane when they observe you in your car seemingly talking to yourself. It is a family matter after all.

The moment you said "I do" to Jesus, He took up your case. You did not have to pay a retainer fee. He is your Advocate, your Attorney General.

You do not need permission to call Him. Just tell Him anything that comes to your mind. He already knows what you are thinking.

Your call will never go to a voice mail.

He is never busy.

He will hold everything you tell Him in confidence.

He will never leave you.

You have a Wonderful Counselor, in the person of Holy Spirit!

He is waiting for your call because He promised in Jeremiah 33:3, "Call to me and I will answer you. I will tell you marvelous and wondrous things that you could never figure out on your own."

CONCLUSION

I know you have been itching to ask what you need to get this license. Do you need:

- elbow grease
- degrees
- an ascetic lifestyle
- to do good
- the list goes on …

Do you have your baskets ready? They have to be empty though. I mean you need to be empty before you can take in, right? I know you also want to know how to empty your baskets.

They are filled with:

- lust
- greed
- gluttony
- envy

- pride
- old habits
- new habits
- fornication
- adultery
- abortion
- gossip

Now empty all that garbage into the incinerator. Don't you want to know that they have all been taken care of once and for all? All is well. One more thing though.

Did that hurt you, emptying all that junk? Wait for the good news. Blessed be the One who has called you and knows exactly when you will accept His invitation.

Now, open your mouth and confess your sins before Him who has the power to wash away your sins. Confess Him as Lord and Savior. Speak to Him from the side of your bed or from the corner of your mouth. If you feel bold right now, shout that *Jesus is Lord*! The angelic hosts are blowing their trumpets right now, welcoming you into God's kingdom. Do you feel a peace come over you? It is the power that raised Jesus up from the dead that is in you making you do cartwheels. Okay, not quite. Get your tissues, and wipe your tears away because they are tears of joy. You have been grafted into a lineage of royals. *You belong!* Your name has been changed forever. Your license is now officially yours. You are equipped to do great and mighty things in the name of Jesus. . You have been chosen!

What's in your basket? Let's see here:

- joy
- peace
- wisdom
- prosperity
- protection
- self-control

- endurance
- temperance
- perseverance
- long-suffering
- long life
- abundant life
- victory
- deliverance
- eternal life

Is your basket full yet? It has to overflow because you have to bless others with God's blessings that make rich and won't add any sorrow.

Show me your license to have a remarkable life of victorious living in … *Him*, the glorious Alpha and Omega, the Great I Am that I Am.

I pray your indulgence right now. Make for yourself an ISP, an individual spiritual plan. Put that in your shopping cart as you travel this journey toward Christian maturity and growth. Ask for wisdom today.

Ask for hitch-free directions.

Ask for favor.

Ask for peace.

Ask for joy.

Ask and you receive, seek and you shall find, knock and it shall be opened to you.

My Prayer

Almighty God, I come to you in the name of Jesus.

I thank You for giving me the opportunity to birth this baby You planted in me.

I thank You for all the babies in me that are yet unborn.

I thank You for trusting me with this task of helping in the remodeling process of Your beloved reading this book right now.

I thank You for the opportunity to share my testimonies.

I thank You for letting me become transparent before the whole world as many come to know You as You have revealed Yourself to me.

I am deeply grateful, Daddy.

I thank You for the desire to want to do Your will.

I thank You for the power you have unleashed in me to do exploits for Your kingdom.

I thank You for all the times You told me to wait.

And I thank You for all the times You told me *no.*

And I thank You for saying *yes* to the things that actually count.

I thank You for making me a ready writer.

I thank You for being my Burden Bearer and allowing me to travel light.

I have traded my sorrow, sickness, disease, pain, shame, depression, divorce, curse, sin, despondency, fears, failures, bad habits, pressures of daily living, present mistakes, past mistakes, and future mistakes.

Your Prayer

Ask God to forgive you of your sins.

Ask Him to take you as you are.

Trade every negative thought you have for the joy of God in Jesus Christ.

You have a treasure in you, waiting to be tapped.

Let the Holy Spirit unlock it in you today.

Reach out … to *Him.*

Empty yourself … in *Him.*

Lift up your voice to … *Him.*

Embrace … *Him.*

As I travel with my hand in Yours, I feel I can scale walls, because You have my back. As You sent Jesus, so have You sent me.

I thank You for trusting me with this assignment. I thank You for the loud voice You have given me to speak of Your love, unmerited favor, joy, peace, and mercy. I have been walking the walk of faith for a long time. I just didn't see any hope. But I am ready to trust You one more time. The thoughts assail me. The questions bombard me. Is it possible that You will give me another chance? I hear You answering me, "Come, My daughter. I feel your pain, My son. I feel your shame. But you see, the price for your sin has been *paid in full!*"

Just by the shed blood of my Jesus whom you confess as *Lord* and *Savior*!

My Prayer (Continued)

Dear God,

My heart bubbles with joy for the salvation of this reader who has taken the invitation to seek to know You more.

Blessed be the name of the Most High.

I thank You, Lord.

You have promised you will always look out for those who put their trust in You.

You have never failed me, Lord.

I place this son or daughter in Your able hands.

You will take good care until Your purpose for their lives is done on earth.

I thank You for all the tests and trials that You walked me through.

Holy Spirit, I pray that You will reside in the one who is reading this book.

Occupy every space in their lives to the praise and glory of Your name.

I bow before Your throne of grace.

I lift up every need before You.

Meet them at the point of their needs, Father God, in the name of Jesus I pray.

Release Your power into your children as they trust You.

It shall be well with Your children, my Lord.

Amen.

Whoever is reading this book, I love you with the love of Jesus.